**Collins**

## Pupil Book 4

# Comprehension Skills

Author: Abigail Steel

William Collins' dream of knowledge for all began with the publication of his first book in 1819.

A self-educated mill worker, he not only enriched millions of lives, but also founded a flourishing publishing house. Today, staying true to this spirit, Collins books are packed with inspiration, innovation and practical expertise. They place you at the centre of a world of possibility and give you exactly what you need to explore it.

Collins. Freedom to teach.

Published by Collins
An imprint of HarperCollins*Publishers*
The News Building
1 London Bridge Street
London
SE1 9GF

HarperCollins*Publishers*
1st Floor, Watermarque Building,
Ringsend Road, Dublin 4, Ireland

Browse the complete Collins catalogue at
**www.collins.co.uk**

© HarperCollins*Publishers* Limited 2017

10 9 8 7 6

ISBN 978-0-00-823637-3

British Library Cataloguing in Publication Data

A Catalogue record for this publication is available from the British Library
Publishing Director: Lee Newman
Publishing Manager: Helen Doran
Senior Editor: Hannah Dove
Project Manager: Emily Hooton
Author: Abigail Steel
Development Editor: Hannah Hirst-Dunton
Copy-editor: Ros and Chris Davies
Proofreader: Gaynor Spry
Cover design and artwork: Amparo Barrera and Ken Vail Graphic Design
Internal design concept: Amparo Barrera
Typesetter: Jouve India Private Ltd
Illustrations: Eva Morales, Dante Ginevra, Andres Avery, Aptara and QBS
Production Controller: Rachel Weaver
Printed and bound by Martins the Printers

## Acknowledgements

The publishers wish to thank the following for permission to reproduce content. Every effort has been made to trace copyright holders and to obtain their permission for the use of copyright materials. The publishers will gladly receive any information enabling them to rectify any error or omission at the first opportunity.

David Higham Associates Ltd for the poem on page 7 'I Love Our Orange Tent' by Berlie Doherty from *Story Chest: Poet's Corner – Big Bulgy Fat Black Slugs*, Thomas Nelson, 1993. Reproduced by permission of David Higham Associates Ltd; HarperCollins Publishers Ltd and David Higham Associates Ltd for an extract on page 22 from *Cockadoodle-Doo, Mr Sultana!* by Michael Morpurgo, HarperCollins Children's Books, 2010, pp.36–46, copyright © 2010 Michael Morpurgo and Shoo Rayner. Reproduced by permission of HarperCollins Publishers Ltd and David Higham Associates Ltd; HarperCollins Publishers Ltd for an extract on page 25 from *Aladdin and the Genies* by Vivian French, copyright © 2016 Vivian French, and an extract on page 31 from *Stowaway!* by Julian Jarman, copyright © 2007 Julian Jarman, and an extract on page 34 from *In the Rue Bel Tesoro* by Lin Coghlan, copyright © 2011 Lin Coghlan. Reproduced by permission of HarperCollins Publishers Ltd; Oxford University Press for an extract on page 37 from *The War Orphan* by Rachel Anderson, Oxford University Press, 2000, copyright © Rachel Anderson 2000. Reproduced by permission of Oxford University Press; Tunji Beier for the poem on page 40 'Kob Antelope' translated by Ulli Beier. Reproduced by kind permission; Andersen Press Ltd for an extract on page 43 from *Angry Arthur* by Hiawyn Oram, 1982. Reproduced with permission; Wes Magee for the poem on page 53 'What is ... the Sun?' from *The Witch's Brew and Other Poems* by Wes Magee, Cambridge University Press, 1989. Reproduced by permission of the author Wes Magee; HarperCollins Publishers Ltd for an extract on page 49 from *Extreme Sports* by Adrian Bradbury, copyright © 2011 Adrian Bradbury, and the poem on page 55 'Whale Alert' from *Jaws and Claws and Things with Wings* by Valerie Bloom, copyright © 2013 Valerie Bloom, and an extract on page 58 from *Cave Wars* by Gillian Cross, copyright © 2011 Gillian Cross, and an extract on page 61 from *Sophie's Rules* by Keith West, copyright © 2011 HarperCollins Publishers Ltd, and an extract on page 64 from *Black Holes* by Anna Claybourne, copyright © 2013 Anna Claybourne, and an extract on page 67 from *Tiger Dead! Tiger Dead! Stories from the Caribbean* by Grace Nichols and John Agard, copyright © 2009 Grace Nichols and John Agard, and the poem on page 70 'Feeding the Ducks' from *Mind the Gap* by Roger McGough, copyright © 2011 Roger McGough. Reproduced by permission of HarperCollins Publishers Ltd.

The publishers would like to thank the following for permission to reproduce photographs: p.4 (t) Gregar Rozac/Alamy Stock Photo, p.4 (c) Martin Bennett/Alamy Stock Photo, p.49 (t) Robert Holmes/Getty Images, p.49 (b) Markson Sparks/REX/Shutterstock, p.64 (t) Hulton Archive/Getty Images and Makena Stock Media/Getty Images.

# Contents

# Non-fiction (web page): Thrills City

Home | About | Plan a visit | What's on | Our rides | Restaurants

**THRILLS CITY ADVENTURE PARK**

Scariest rides ever:

The Brazen Beast | Techno Ride | Raging River's Revenge | Mighty Meteor | Vortex

An awesome day for all the family

- Escape on a once-in-a-lifetime adventure
- Unlimited fun all year round
- New this year – embark on an underwater adventure in the new sea-life aquarium
- Over the Rainbow Club – fab fun for our younger guests
- Live entertainment and characters
- Surprises at every turn
- Splash yourself silly in the water park!
- Stay overnight at our special 4 ★ family-friendly hotel
- Relax in our spa and health club

## SPECIAL OFFERS

2-for-1 tickets before 13 July

Family Weekend Autumn Saver

Jump the queues and save 5% – print your tickets at home

## OFFERS BY EMAIL

Sign up now to receive the latest information and offers and become a Select Guest

Title:
Surname:
Email:

Sign up

Open 10 a.m. to 6 p.m. every day ★ Close to motorway ★ Free parking

## Get started

Copy these sentences carefully and complete them by filling in the gaps. Use the text from the web page to find the answers.

1. Thrills City has a club for younger guests called the _____ _____ _____ _____.

2. Guests might want to relax in the spa and _____ _____.

3. You can have fun swimming in the _____ _____.

4. If you sign up now for information and offers to be sent by email, you will become a _____ _____.

5. You can watch live entertainment and meet _____.

## Try these

Write a sentence to answer each question. One has been done for you.

1. Where would you click to learn more about events happening at Thrills City?

   Answer: *I would click on the 'What's on' button to learn more about events happening at Thrills City.*

2. How could you save money when buying tickets for a trip to Thrills City in June? Give both ways.

3. Could you visit the park on a Sunday? How do you know this?

4. Could you get something to eat there? Why do you think this?

5. What would be a good way to get there? Why do you think this?

## Now try these

1. Imagine you are planning to visit Thrills City. What other information might you want to know? Write down your questions and make notes about where on this website you might find the answers.

2. Pretend you have clicked on the 'Plan a visit' button. Design the 'Plan a visit' web page.

3. Think about how the information on this web page might be presented if it were a leaflet rather than a web page. Would the different web pages be different pages in the leaflet, or just different sections on a larger page? Would you add a map? When you have thought about this, design the leaflet.

# Poetry: 'I Love Our Orange Tent'

I love our orange tent.
We plant it like a flower in the field.
The grass smells sweet inside it.
And at night
When we're lying in it,
I hear the owl crying.

When the wind blows,
my tent flaps
like a flying bird.

And the rain
patters down on it
with tiny footsteps.

I feel warm and safe
inside my tent.

But when the sun shines,
that's when I love it best!

When I wake up
and the sun is shining,
it pours in like yellow honey.
It glows like gold.
I love our orange tent.

**Berlie Doherty**

## Get started

Copy these sentences carefully and complete them by filling in the gaps. Use the poem to find the answers.

1. The poet sets up the tent in a _____.

2. At _____, she can hear an owl.

3. She can also hear the _____ dripping onto it.

4. She loves it best when _____ _____ _____.

5. The sun makes the tent _____ like gold.

## Try these

Write a sentence to answer each question. One has been done for you.

1.  What can the poet hear when she is in the tent?

    Answer: *When she is in the tent, the poet can hear an owl crying, the tent flapping and the rain pattering.*

2.  Which other senses does the poet use to describe her experiences with the tent?

3.  The words 'like a flower' are a simile. In your own words, explain what a simile is. Use a dictionary to help you if necessary.

4.  Write down the three other similes in the poem.

5.  Does the poet go camping on her own? Why do you think this?

## Now try these

1.  Why do you think the line 'I love our orange tent' is repeated at the beginning and the end of the poem? What effect does the repetition have on you as a reader?

2.  Imagine you are the poet, camping in the orange tent. Write a short diary entry about what you can see, hear, smell and feel. Your diary entry should contain some new ideas. It should not be a poem.

3.  Think about something you love doing. Use four similes of your own to describe what it is like.

# Poetry: 'The Donkey'

I saw a donkey
One day old,
His head was too big
For his neck to hold;
His legs were shaky
And long and loose,
They rocked and staggered
And weren't much use.

He tried to gambol
And frisk a bit,
But he wasn't quite sure
Of the trick of it.
His queer little coat
Was soft and grey,
And curled at his neck
In a lovely way.

His face was wistful
And left no doubt
That he felt life needed
Some thinking about.
So he blundered round
In venturesome quest,
And then lay flat
On the ground to rest.

He looked so little
And weak and slim,
I prayed the world
Might be good to him.

**Anon**

## Get started

Copy these sentences and complete them by filling in the gaps. Use the poem to find the answers.

1. The donkey was _____ _____ old.
2. His _____ seemed too small for his _____.
3. He had a soft, grey _____.
4. The poet thought the donkey's face looked _____.
5. Eventually, the donkey lay down to _____ on the ground.

## Try these

Write a sentence to answer each question. One has been done for you.

1. Why couldn't the donkey move around well?

   Answer: *The donkey couldn't move around well because it was very young and just learning to walk.*

2. Explain the meanings of the words 'gambol', 'frisk', 'blundered', 'venturesome' and 'quest'. Use a dictionary for help if necessary.

3. What do the words you explained make you think about the donkey's attitude?

4. How do you think the poet felt about the donkey? Why do you think this?

5. Why do you think the poet 'prayed the world might be good to him'?

### Now try these

1. The poet believes that the donkey 'felt life needed some thinking about'. Imagine the donkey can put these thoughts into words. Note down some questions he might like to ask and ideas about what he might hope to do next.

2. Find the seven pairs of rhyming words. Look at how the rhymes are arranged. Then write one new verse about the donkey using the same arrangement of rhymes.

3. Draw a picture of the donkey trying to gambol. Use the poem to help you make your drawing detailed.

# Non-fiction (newspaper report): The Accident

## LATEST NEWS

# SECOND ICE FATALITY IN A WEEK

Tragedy struck again yesterday when an elderly lady fell through the ice. Mrs Wills, of Onslow Gardens, had been walking alone with her sister's dog when it chased a duck onto the frozen river. It is the first time in living memory that the River Thames has frozen from bank to bank.

Onlookers struggled desperately to save Mrs Wills, 79, when she fell through the ice while trying to rescue the black Labrador. Rescue services were on the scene within five minutes, but as Chief Officer Chung said, "There was no way anyone could survive more than a minute or two in water with sub-zero temperatures." Last week, the same rescue crew tried unsuccessfully to rescue an eight-year-old boy who had been playing on the ice.

## Get started

Copy these sentences carefully and complete them by filling in the gaps. Use the newspaper report to find the answers.

1. Yesterday, an elderly lady fell through the _____.

2. The River _____ had frozen over.

3. Mrs Wills lived in _____ _____.

4. Mrs Wills was _____ years old.

5. The dog was a black _____.

## Try these

Write a sentence to answer each question. One has been done for you.

1. When was the last time someone remembered the River Thames freezing from bank to bank?

   Answer: *Never, as this was the first time in living memory that the River Thames had frozen from bank to bank.*

2. With whom had Mrs Wills been walking?

3. The rescue crew arrived very quickly. Why didn't Mrs Wills survive?

4. Why do you think Mrs Wills went onto the ice?

5. Do you think it would be safe to play on the frozen Thames? Why do you think this?

## Now try these

1. Imagine a news reporter interviewed someone who saw the accident. Write at least three sentences as though this person is saying them, describing what they saw.

2. Write two extra paragraphs for the newspaper report. One could contain the interview with the person who saw the accident. One could add extra information: did the rescue crew save the dog? Use dramatic language and clear descriptions to match the style of the newspaper report.

3. Design a poster that could be displayed to warn people of the dangers of frozen rivers. What might people need to know? Use some of the information from the newspaper report to help you.

# Non-fiction (diary): Holiday diary

### Holiday diary

### Friday 2 August

Bored, bored, bored! This is our holiday, so you'd think it would be fun. Huh! Raj just sits playing games on his phone all day – he might as well not be on holiday at all, because he doesn't seem to want to go out or play or do anything interesting. Mum and Dad are so exhausted (apparently) that all they really want to do is flop. Still, they've promised to take me to the beach this afternoon. Maybe there'll be someone to play with there.

### Later …

The beach was brilliant! It's really wide, flat and sandy. The sand is excellent for running on, and also for digging and making sandcastles. I had a great time, but you'll never guess what the best thing was. I made friends with this really nice girl, Stacey. She's coming over to our holiday house tomorrow to play.

### Saturday 3 August

Today was just … amazing. I'm still trying to work out how I feel about it actually. Stacey came over, and we were playing a great game in the garden of the holiday house, when we noticed a little plane flying overhead. It seemed to be flying a bit low, but we didn't really think about it – until we suddenly saw clouds of smoke billowing out of the back of it! Then, suddenly, it dropped down into the sea. The pilot of the plane must have pressed the 'eject' button because we could see him floating down by parachute. Stacey and I just stared at each other. We were in shock. Then Stacey realised we had to phone for help.

"Meena!" she said. "Grab the phone and dial 999. We need Air-Sea Rescue!" I quickly got on the phone, and told the lady where we were and what we had seen. The lady said they would send a helicopter at once. Sure enough, within minutes we saw a big orange helicopter hovering over the sea where the plane had crashed. A rescue worker was lowered down on a rope, and grabbed the pilot of the plane, who was clinging to the wreckage. Then the pair of them got winched up into the helicopter and flew away.

I hope the pilot is OK. Mum says Stacey and I probably saved his life.

## Get started

Copy these sentences and complete them by filling in the gaps. Use the diary entry to find the answers.

1. The girl writing the diary is called _____.

2. Her mum and dad felt _____ on Friday.

3. Raj didn't want to do _____ interesting.

4. The two girls met on _____ afternoon.

5. Stacey went to Meena's holiday house on _____.

## Try these

Write a sentence to answer each question. One has been done for you.

1. How did the girls know the pilot ejected?

   Answer: *The girls knew the pilot ejected because they could see him floating down by parachute.*

2. Who arrived to help the pilot?

3. Who do you think Raj is? Why do you think this?

4. How do you think Meena will feel about what happened on Saturday when she works it out?

5. How do you think Meena's mum feels about what happened? Why do you think this?

## Now try these

1. How do you think Stacey feels about what happened since she met Meena? Write at least three sentences as though Stacey is saying them.

2. Write Meena's diary entry for the next day. What might she and Stacey do? Is Raj more interested in joining in? Remember to use diary features.

3. Imagine you are Meena or Stacey, and that Air-Sea Rescue has asked you to draw a picture of what you saw. Make sure all the details from the extract are in the picture.

# Fiction (fable): 'The Eagle and the Turtle'

**'The Eagle and the Turtle' – a fable by Aesop**

The Turtle was not satisfied with his life. He wanted to stop being a turtle.

"I'm tired of swimming about in the sea and crawling about on the beach, getting nowhere in particular," he grumbled. "I want to be able to fly in the air like an eagle."

He spoke to the Eagle about it.

"You're not built for flying," the Eagle told the Turtle. "You haven't any wings."

"Don't worry about that," answered the Turtle. "I've watched how the birds do it. I've watched them soar and glide, skim and dive. Even if I haven't got wings, I can make my four flippers act like four stout oars in the air, the way I do in the water. Just get me up there, and you'll see I can fly as well as any of the birds – probably better! Besides, if you'll carry me as high as the clouds, I'll bring you lots of rare pearls from the sea."

The Eagle was tempted, and carried the Turtle up to a great height.

"Now, then!" cried the Eagle. "Fly!"

But the moment the Turtle was on his own, he fell from the sky. He fell like a stone, and on a stone he landed. He struck with such force that he smashed into little pieces.

**Moral: Be satisfied with what you are.**

## Get started

Copy these sentences carefully and complete them by filling in the gaps. Use the fable to find the answers.

1. The Turtle was not _____ with being a turtle.

2. He was _____ of swimming about in the sea.

3. He decided to speak to the _____ about his problem.

4. The Eagle told the Turtle he wasn't _____ for flying.

5. But the Turtle insisted the Eagle carry him as high as the _____.

## Try these

Write a sentence to answer each question. One has been done for you.

1. Why was the Turtle unhappy with his life?

   Answer: *The Turtle was unhappy with his life because he was tired of getting nowhere in particular.*

2. Which part of his body did the Turtle think would be as good as wings?

3. In your own words, explain the moral of the story.

4. Why do you think the Eagle agreed to carry the Turtle into the clouds?

5. What do you think the Eagle expected to happen? Why do you think this?

## Now try these

1. What might the Eagle really think of the Turtle? Write three sentences as though the Eagle is saying them.

2. Rewrite the extract from the Eagle's point of view. What parts of the story will change?

3. Draw a picture of the Turtle talking to the Eagle. Add thought bubbles to show what they are each thinking.

# Fiction (classic): 'Cockadoodle-Doo, Mr Sultana!'

**From 'Cockadoodle-Doo, Mr Sultana!' by Michael Morpurgo**

Out in the countryside, the little red rooster was scratching around in the dusty farm track at the edge of the cornfield.

He scratched and he scratched. Suddenly there was something strange in the earth, something different, something very pretty that glistened and shone and twinkled in the sun. He tried eating it, but it didn't taste very good. So he dropped it. And then he had a sudden and brilliant idea.

"I know," he said to himself. "Poor old mistress mine loves pretty things. She's always saying so, and she's got nothing pretty of her own. I'll take it home for her. Then she won't be cross with me for running away, will she?"

But just as he picked it up again, along the farm track came the great fat Sultan on his horse, and in front of him, dozens of his servants, all of them crawling on their hands and knees in the dirt.

Closer and closer they came. All at once they spotted the little red rooster *and* the diamond button too, glinting in his beak.

"There my lord Sultan!" they cried. "LOOK! That little red rooster. He's got your diamond button."

"So that's what it is," the little red rooster said to himself.

The great fat Sultan rode up, scattering his servants hither and thither as he came. "Little Red Rooster," he said from high up on his horse. "I see you have my diamond button.

I am your great and mighty Sultan. Give it to me at once. It's valuable, very valuable. And it's *mine*."

"I don't think so, Mr Sultana," replied the little red rooster, who had never in his life been frightened of anyone or anything. "COCKADOODLE-DOO, Mr Sultana. Finders keepers. If it's so valuable, then I'm going to give it to poor mistress mine. She needs it a lot more than you, I think. Sorry, Mr Sultana."

"*What*!" spluttered the Sultan. "Mr Sultana? How dare you speak to me like that? How dare you? Did you hear what that infernal bird called me? Fetch me that rooster. Fetch me my diamond button! Grab him! Grab that rooster!"

There was a frightful kerfuffle of dust and feathers … and SQUAWKING, as the Sultan's servants tried to grab the little red rooster. Whatever they did, they just could not catch him. In the end, the little red rooster ran off into the cornfield. But although he'd escaped their clutches, he was very cross with himself, for in all the kerfuffle he had dropped the diamond button.

## Get started

Copy these sentences carefully and complete them by filling in the gaps. Use the story to find the answers.

1. The main character of this story is the little _____ _____.

2. He found something shiny on the dusty _____ _____ by the cornfield.

3. The shiny item was a _____ _____.

4. The button belonged to the _____.

5. The rooster ran away into the _____, but he dropped the button!

## Try these

Write a sentence to answer each question. One has been done for you.

1. Why did the Sultan want the button back?

   Answer: *The Sultan wanted the button back because it was very valuable.*

2. What is a 'sultan'? What is a 'sultana'? Use a dictionary for help if necessary. What do you think a 'kerfuffle' is?

3. Find three reasons the little red rooster wanted to give the item to his mistress.

4. How do you think the little red rooster felt when he was asked to give the button back?

5. Do you think the Sultan expected this response? Why do you think this?

## Now try these

1. How do you think the Sultan feels now? Write three sentences as though the Sultan is saying them.

2. Write a different ending, where the rooster doesn't lose the button. What do you think the rooster's mistress would do if he took it to her?

3. Draw a picture of the confrontation between the Sultan and the little red rooster. Use speech bubbles to show what they are saying to each other. Add some thought bubbles to show what the Sultan's servants think.

# Fiction: 'Aladdin and the Genies'

**From 'Aladdin and the Genies' by Vivian French**

**Chapter 1**

*WANTED! Clever young boy who wants to be rich! Must be willing to obey orders without asking questions. If interested, knock on the blue door in the street of camels.*

*Signed: Kadar Ghazi the merchant*

The notice was pinned on the town gate. Aladdin read it carefully. "I want to be rich," he said. "And I don't ask many questions."

"Yes, you do," said his mother. "You're always asking questions!"

"I can pretend I don't," Aladdin told her. "And then we can afford some food. I'm starving!"

His mother shook her head. "We don't know anything about this Kadar Ghazi."

"Don't worry," Aladdin said. "I'm very clever, remember!"

His mother sighed. "Be careful."

**Chapter 2**

Trying not to feel too hopeful, Aladdin soon found the blue door. He knocked, and the door opened … but there was nobody there.

Aladdin strode inside. The room was dark and empty. There were no cushions and no rugs … just a bare stone floor. Wondering what would happen next, he decided to wait for a while.

"Aren't you afraid?" a deep voice echoed around the room.

"No," Aladdin said. "I can't see anything to be afraid of."

"Good!" said the voice. A door in the wall swung open, and an enormous man dressed in shimmering silk appeared.

"He looks extremely wealthy," Aladdin thought.

"I'm Kadar Ghazi," the man growled. "Who are you?"

## Get started

Copy these sentences carefully and complete them by filling in the gaps.

1. The notice was _____ on the town gate.

2. "We don't _____ _____ about this Kadar Ghazi."

3. Trying not to feel too hopeful, Aladdin soon found the _____ _____.

4. Wondering what would happen next, he _____ to wait for a while.

5. A door in the wall swung open, and an _____ man dressed in shimmering silk appeared.

## Try these

Write a sentence to answer each question. One has been done for you.

1. Who placed the notice?

   Answer: *Kadar Ghazi the merchant placed the notice.*

2. Who was the notice designed to find?

3. How is Aladdin suitable for the job? How is he unsuitable?

4. Why do you think Aladdin's mother wants him to be careful?

5. What do you think was the purpose of the dark and empty room?

## Now try these

1. What might Kadar Ghazi have thought about Aladdin at first? Write three sentences as though Kadar Ghazi is thinking them.

2. Rewrite Chapter 1 as if Aladdin's mother is describing what happened. What parts of the chapter will you change?

3. Draw a picture of Aladdin talking to Kadar Ghazi. Add speech bubbles to show what they might say next.

# Fiction (classic): 'The Wind in the Willows'

**From 'The Wind in the Willows' by Kenneth Grahame**

The Mole, who had been busily spring-cleaning his house, had come out for a rest.

As he sat on the grass and looked across the river, a dark hole in the bank opposite, just above the water's edge, caught his eye. Something bright and small seemed to twinkle down in the heart of it, vanish, then twinkle once more like a tiny star. But it could hardly be a star in such an unlikely situation, and it was too glittering and too small for a glow-worm. Then, as he looked, it winked at him, and so declared itself to be an eye, and a small face began gradually to grow up round it, like a frame round a picture. A brown little face, with whiskers.
A grave round face, with the same twinkle in its eye that had first attracted his notice. Small neat ears and thick silky hair. It was the Water Rat!

The Rat said nothing, but stooped and unfastened a rope and hauled on it, then lightly stepped into a little boat which the Mole had not observed. It was painted blue outside and white within, and was just the size for two animals, and the Mole's whole heart went out to it at once, even though he did not yet fully understand its uses.

The Rat sculled smartly across and made fast. Then he held up his fore-paw as the Mole stepped gingerly down. "Lean on that!" he said. "Now then, step lively!" and the Mole to his surprise and rapture found himself actually seated in the stern of a real boat.

"This has been a wonderful day!" he said, as the Rat shoved off and took to the sculls again. "Do you know, I've never been in a boat before in all my life."

## Get started

Copy these sentences carefully and complete them by filling in the gaps. Use the story to find the answers.

1. The Mole had needed a rest from
   _____-_____ his house.

2. He was sitting on the grass next to the _____.

3. The Water Rat had silky hair and small neat
   _____.

4. The boat was just the size for
   _____ _____.

5. The Mole had _____
   been in a boat before.

Write a sentence to answer each question. One has been done for you.

1. Why couldn't the Mole see the Water Rat's eye properly at first?

   Answer: *The Mole couldn't see the Water Rat's eye properly at first because the Water Rat was in a dark hole.*

2. What do the words 'stooped', 'hauled', 'sculled' and 'rapture' mean? Use a dictionary for help if necessary.

3. How did the Mole feel about being in the boat?

4. Did the Mole expect the Water Rat to invite him onto the boat? How do you know?

5. Do you think the Mole and the Water Rat already knew each other? Why do you think that?

## Now try these

1. What might the Water Rat have thought about the Mole at first? Write three sentences as though the Water Rat is thinking them.

2. Rewrite the extract from the Water Rat's point of view.

3. Draw a detailed picture of the Water Rat sculling towards the Mole.

# Fiction (historical): 'Stowaway!'

This historical adventure tells the story of a young Tudor boy in the 16th century, and his dream to sail with the famous Captain Francis Drake.

**From 'Stowaway!' by Julia Jarman**

How Dickon envied his best friend, Tib, who was aboard the 'Pelican', for the famous Francis Drake was its Captain – Francis Drake, England's greatest sailor and friend of Good Queen Bess. Francis Drake who had come back from the Spanish Main, his ship laden with gold. And now he was setting out on another exciting voyage – with Tib as his cabin boy.

Dickon gritted his teeth to stop the tears. He'd tried to get a job, but the second mate had taken one look at his lame leg and said, "Sorry, lad. We only take the fit and able. You couldn't climb the mainmast."

"I could …" But the second mate hadn't listened. Instead, he said to Tib, "You'll do. You look a strong lad." So Tib would have gold for his mother when the ship returned to Plymouth. Dickon would have nothing, and his poor widowed mother had eight boys to feed.

Dickon was suddenly jolted out of his misery by a loud voice. "Here, boy, carry this!" A young gentleman in a leather doublet had dropped a bag at Dickon's feet.

Then a gentleman with dark hair and beard called out from the 'Pelican'.

"Cousin John! Not a moment too soon. We sail at five!" Dickon couldn't believe his eyes. It was Francis Drake! It must be. He wore a gold chain round his neck.

"Cousin Francis!" The young gentleman ran up the gangway. Dickon ran after him, carrying the bag. He could run and climb. He could do lots of things.

## Get started

Copy these sentences and complete them by filling in the gaps. Use the story to find the answers.

1. _____ and _____ were best friends.

2. Francis Drake was the _____ of the 'Pelican'.

3. Tib was Drake's _____ boy.

4. Dickon had a _____ leg.

5. Despite his leg, Dickon knew he could _____ and _____.

## Try these

Write a sentence to answer each question. One has been done for you.

1. Why did the second mate say Dickon couldn't do the job?

   Answer: *The second mate said that Dickon couldn't do the job because Dickon had a lame leg and wouldn't be able to climb the mainmast.*

2. What do the words 'doublet', 'lame' and 'widowed' mean? Use a dictionary for help if necessary. What do the words 'lame' and 'widowed' tell you about the life of Dickon and his family?

3. Who was the man who threw Dickon the bag?

4. What did this man want Dickon to do?

5. Find three pieces of evidence in the text that show it is a historical story.

## Now try these

1. What do you think Dickon will want to know about the ship and the voyage? Write three questions as though Dickon is asking them.

2. Write a diary entry as though Tib is writing it. How do you think Tib feels about the voyage? How did he feel when he thought Dickon would be left behind?

3. Draw a detailed picture of Dickon. Choose whether you will draw him when he thinks he will be left behind, or when he is running with John's bag. Use the extract to help you.

# Playscript: 'In the Rue Bel Tesoro'

This is the beginning of a play about children living in a country where soldiers are fighting and people are struggling to survive.

### From 'In the Rue Bel Tesoro' by Lin Coghlan

### SCENE 1

(A busy train station crowded with travellers. Sasha and Omar arrive pushing an old-fashioned pram and carrying a bag stuffed with belongings.)

SASHA:     Don't say anything, Omar; let me do the talking.

OMAR:     (into the pram)
You've got to keep quiet, Valentine, we're in the station now.

(They approach a soldier checking documents at the entrance to the platform.)

SOLDIER:   Papers?

SASHA:     (handing over the papers)
We're going to meet our mother. She's waiting for us.

SOLDIER:   The baby – his pass?

SASHA:     He's … a new baby, he doesn't have one.

SOLDIER:   No papers, I can't let you through.

(Fran arrives with a huge suitcase and pushes in.)

FRAN:      Please – let an old woman by! My bad hip! My feet!

SOLDIER:   (unmoved)
Papers?

(Fran gives him her papers as the children watch.)

**SOLDIER:** Go through.

(Fran hurries through the barrier. Sasha grabs Omar and drags him after Fran, getting away from the soldier.)

**SOLDIER:** Hey, you! Come back!

(Sasha and Omar disappear into the crowd.)

## SCENE 2

(Fran staggers into the train compartment with her bundles.)

**SASHA:** Please, madam, if we could stay with you, we're on our own …

**FRAN:** Oh no – impossible. I must have my space.

**SASHA:** The soldiers don't stop old people so much when they have children.

**FRAN:** I don't like babies.

**OMAR:** It isn't a baby – it's a dog.

(Sasha looks at him furiously.)

## Get started

Copy these sentences carefully and complete them by filling in the gaps. Use the playscript to find the answers.

1. Scene 1 is set in a busy _____ _____.

2. Sasha and Omar's bag is stuffed with _____.

3. The soldier checks everyone's _____.

4. Fran is an _____ _____.

5. Omar tells Fran they have a _____, not a _____.

## Try these

Write a sentence to answer each question. One has been done for you.

1. Where is Valentine?

   Answer: *Valentine is in the pram.*

2. Why does Sasha want to stay with Fran?

3. Why is Sasha furious with Omar?

4. How do you think the children feel?
   Why might they feel like this?

5. Look at the text from the extract that is in brackets.
   What does this text tell you?

## Now try these

1. What do you know about the place where the children are?
   What would you like to find out in order to understand the
   play better? Write notes about the information
   you already have and the information you
   would like to have.

2. Write a short message from Sasha to her
   mother, telling her about what happened at
   the train station. Try to imagine what events
   and feelings Sasha might want to write about.

3. Rewrite Scene 2 as a chapter from a story
   instead of a playscript. How will you explain
   and describe what is happening?

# Fiction: 'The Day the Helicopters Came'

This story is about how frightening it was for a child when an army invaded a village during the Vietnam War in the 1960s.

### From 'The Day the Helicopters Came' by Rachel Anderson

We had a cow for milk, some hens, and a goat. We harvested enough rice and vegetables for our family and the rest my mother sent downriver to market in the city.

Then one day the helicopters came. We watched them circle, then bump down, one after another in rapid succession, onto our vegetable gardens. The men jumped out and ran, bent double as though themselves afraid of being fired on, over melons, beans, celery, trampling with their boots on whatever produce hadn't already been destroyed by shells. "We must go in," said my mother, and she hurried us inside. But my grandmother was in a trance, dazed by three nights in the shelter. My mother sat her down gently on the stool and gave her the baby to hold while she saw to the clearing up.

The room was suddenly darkened by a huge man, higher than the door lintel, blocking out the light. He was so tall that he had to stoop to stand in the doorway, and even then the top of his helmet was lost in the grass thatch.

"Where's your husband, lady?" he shouted. My mother snatched the baby back from my grandmother and held it to her tightly. The man instinctively twitched his gun back at her. He was very frightened.

"Your husband! Where is he?"

He didn't see me. I was in the folds of my father's jacket hanging on a peg. But as I flattened myself more against the wall I knocked an earthenware dish down from the shelf. It clattered to the floor.

## Get started

Copy these sentences carefully and complete them by filling in the gaps. Use the story to find the answers.

1. The girl's family had a cow because it could give them _____.

2. Her mother sent their spare rice and vegetables to the _____ in the _____.

3. The helicopters landed on the _____ _____.

4. The men jumped out and _____.

5. The girl's mother _____ the family inside.

## Try these

Write a sentence to answer each question. One has been done for you.

1. Why was the girl's grandmother 'in a trance'?

   Answer: *The girl's grandmother was 'in a trance' because she had spent three nights in the shelter.*

2. What do the words 'succession' and 'lintel' mean? In the setting of the extract, what are 'shells'? Use a dictionary for help if necessary.

3. How do you think the soldiers felt as they ran from the helicopter? Why do you think this?

4. The girl says the soldier in the doorway was very frightened. How do you think she knew this?

5. Why do you think the soldiers trampled on the vegetables?

## Now try these

1. How might the girl's grandmother feel about what is happening? Write at least three sentences as though she is saying them.

2. Write at least eight lines of dialogue that might occur next between the girl's mother and the soldier in the doorway. What would they ask each other? Remember to think about how they might feel.

3. Draw a detailed picture of the soldiers running in the vegetable patch. Add a caption to your picture, as though it will be used in a newspaper report.

# Poetry: Humans —Friends or Foes?

Look carefully at this Ragamala painting from medieval India, and read this poem by an unknown Nigerian poet. Both are about the relationship between people and animals.

**'Kob Antelope'**

A creature to pet and spoil like a child.
Smooth-skinned
stepping cautiously in the lemon grass.
Round and plump
like a newly wedded wife.
The neck
heavy with brass rings.
The eyes
gentle like a bird's.
The head
beautiful like carved wood.
When you finally escape
you spread fine dust
like a butterfly shaking its wings.
Your neck seems long
so very long
to the greedy hunter

**Yoruba Poetry compiled
and edited by Ulli Beier**

Todi Ragini
A Ragamala painting

## Get started

Copy these sentences carefully and complete them by filling in the gaps. Use the poem and the painting to find the answers.

1. The poem is about a kob _____.

2. There are five deer and one _____ in the painting.

3. The painting is from _____ and the poem is from _____.

4. The animal in the poem has _____ skin.

5. The animal in the poem has a _____ neck.

## Try these

Write a sentence to answer each question. One has been done for you.

1. Who is the other character mentioned in the poem?

   Answer: *The hunter is the other character mentioned in the poem.*

2. In your own words, explain the way the antelope moves. Use a dictionary for help if necessary.

3. Why do you think the hunter is interested in the antelope? Explain your answer.

4. How do you think the poet feels about the antelope? Why do you think this?

5. Look at the painting. How do you think the woman and the deer feel about each other? Why do you think this?

## Now try these

1. Find three similes in the poem that describe what the antelope is like. Then think about what the deer in the painting are like. Write down at least three similes to describe the deer in the painting.

2. Imagine you are the woman in the painting. Write a poem like 'Kob Antelope' about the deer. Think carefully about your descriptions and what might happen in the forest. Use at least one new simile.

3. Draw a picture of the antelope in a forest. Use ideas from the poem and from the painting. Will you show the hunter? Will you show the poet?

# Fiction: 'Angry Arthur' and Poetry: 'My Hair as Black as Dirty Coal'

Here are two pieces of writing about being angry: one is prose and one is poetry. In 'Angry Arthur', not being allowed to watch his favourite TV programme makes Arthur very, very angry. Bertie Thomson won a prize for his poem about anger when he was nine years old.

### From 'Angry Arthur' by Hiawyn Oram

"No," said his mother, "it's too late. Go to bed."

"I'll get angry," said Arthur.

"Get angry," said his mother.

So he did. Very, very angry.

He got so angry that his anger became a stormcloud exploding thunder and lightning and hailstones.

"That's enough," said his mother. But it wasn't.

Arthur's anger became a hurricane hurling rooftops and chimneys and church spires.

"That's enough," said his father. But it wasn't.

Arthur's anger became a typhoon tipping whole towns into the sea.

"That's enough," said his grandfather. But it wasn't.

Arthur's anger became a universequake and the earth and the moon and the stars and the planets, Arthur's country and Arthur's town, his street, his house, his garden and his bedroom were nothing more than bits in space.

Arthur sat on a bit of Mars and thought. He thought and thought. "Why was I so angry?" he thought. He never did remember. Can you?

### 'My Hair as Black as Dirty Coal'

My hair as black as dirty coal,
My eyes sizzle like fried eggs in a pan,
My nose breathes heavily like a charging wild bull.
Because:

(My brother …)

My mouth breathing fire like a dragon.
My stomach going in and out,
I clench my fists hard like compressing a lemon
Until all the juice comes out.

(kicked my …)

My anger bubbling inside,
Ready to fire out of my head.
I think I'm Arnold
Schwarzenegger.
My feet heat up ready to kick out
And then I burst out.

(ball over the fence!!)

**Bertie Thomson**

## Get started

Copy these sentences carefully and complete them by filling in the gaps. Use the story and the poem to find the answers.

1. Arthur's anger first became a _____ exploding thunder.

2. It then hurled rooftops and _____ and _____ _____.

3. Arthur was angry because his mother said he couldn't watch a _____ _____.

4. The poet was breathing like a _____ _____ bull.

5. His feet heat up ready to _____ out.

## Try these

Write a sentence to answer each question. One has been done for you.

1. How are the two extracts similar?

   Answer: *The two extracts are similar because they are both about anger.*

2. What is the effect of the words in brackets in the poem?

3. Find four similes in the poem.

4. The words 'his anger became a stormcloud' are a metaphor. In your own words, explain what a metaphor is. Use a dictionary for help.

5. What are hurricanes and typhoons? Use a dictionary for help if necessary. What do you think a 'universequake' is? Explain how these words help you to imagine Arthur's anger.

## Now try these

1. Why do you think these writers use similes and metaphors? What effect do they have on you as a reader?

2. How do you think the poet's brother feels? Write down at least three ideas for similes that explain how he might be feeling.

3. Imagine feeling very happy. Write a paragraph that uses metaphors to show what your happiness is like. If you need to, use the 'Angry Arthur' story for ideas about how to write your metaphors.

# Non-fiction (information text): 'Feathered Record Breakers'

**Feathered Record Breakers**

**Biggest alive**

The giant of the bird world is the ostrich, from Africa. It grows up to 2.7 metres and can weigh over 155 kilograms. Its eggs are also the biggest, weighing in at 1.5 kilograms.

**Heaviest extinct bird**

The roc, or elephant bird, lived in Madagascar until 300 years ago. It weighed over 420 kilograms, and laid eggs seven times as big as the ostrich.

**Heaviest flier**

The African Kori bustard has been known to weigh 18 kilograms.

**Tallest extinct bird**

Some species of the New Zealand moa grew to over 4 metres, but they died out about 700 years ago.

**Fastest flier**

Spine-tailed swifts can reach 170 kilometres per hour.

**Fastest runner**

Ostriches can run at 65 kilometres per hour.

### Greatest wingspan

The wandering albatross has a wingspan up to 3 metres.

### Smallest bird

The bee hummingbird measures less than 6 centimetres from beak to tail and weighs 2 grams.

### Deepest divers

Emperor penguins have been known to reach depths of over 250 metres.

## Get started

Copy these sentences carefully and complete them by filling in the gaps. Use the facts to find the answers.

1. The fastest flier is the _____-_____ _____.

2. Emperor penguins have dived over _____ _____ deep.

3. The biggest bird alive is the _____.

4. A bee hummingbird weighs only _____ _____.

5. The roc weighed over _____ _____.

## Try these

Write a sentence to answer each question. Use the text to help you. One has been done for you.

1. Which bird holds two of these records? Which records does it hold?

   Answer: *The ostrich holds two of these records: the biggest bird alive and the fastest runner.*

2. What does 'wingspan' mean? Use a dictionary for help if necessary. Which of the birds in the extract do you think has the smallest wingspan?

3. Do the facts tell you whether the ostrich or the roc was taller? If so, which was taller?

4. Why do you think the author included birds that are extinct?

5. Why do you think this text uses subheadings?

## Now try these

1. In your own words, write three different facts about birds. If you can, discover interesting new facts by doing some research.

2. Which feathered record breaker do you think is the most interesting? Write a paragraph to tell someone else about this bird, explaining why you think it is the most interesting.

3. Draw a picture of an ostrich with its eggs. Label it with information boxes, using the details given in the text.

# Non-fiction (information text): 'Extreme Sports'

**From 'Extreme Sports' by Adrian Bradbury**

**What are extreme sports?**

Extreme sports involve all the action, adventure, thrills and heartaches of other sports, but with added risks. Extreme sportsmen and sportswomen push themselves to the limit. If they go fast, they want to go faster. If they climb high, they want to climb higher. If they find something easy, they want to make it more difficult. They want to challenge themselves, even if it means facing much greater dangers than in ordinary sports.

Most extreme sports are physically tough, so their sportsmen and sportswomen tend to be younger rather than older, but fitness, skill, balance and, above all, training and experience are more important than age.

**Fly like a bird**

All airborne extreme sports are at the mercy of the weather, which can change quickly and dramatically. Anyone taking part in these sports must decide if they have the skill and experience to cope with the conditions. *Is it safe to jump or fly?*

### Skydiving

Parachutes were first used as a way of escaping safely from a hot-air balloon. Their design and safety improved during the 20th century and jumpers began to use parachutes for sport.

In a typical skydive, the jumpers will leap from a plane at an altitude of 3,962 metres. They'll open their parachutes 610 metres above the ground after a freefall of one minute.

## Get started

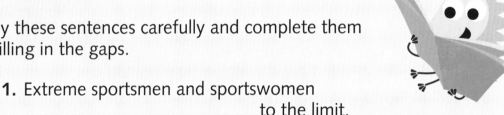

Copy these sentences carefully and complete them by filling in the gaps.

1. Extreme sportsmen and sportswomen _____ _____ to the limit.

2. If they climb high, they want to _____ higher.

3. If they find _____ easy, they want to make it more difficult.

4. They want to challenge themselves, even if it means facing much greater _____ than in ordinary sports.

5. Parachutes were first used as a way of _____ safely from a hot-air balloon.

## Try these

Write a sentence to answer each question. One has been done for you.

1. Why do extreme sportsmen and sportswomen tend to be younger rather than older?

Answer: *Extreme sportsmen and sportswomen tend to be younger rather than older because most extreme sports are physically tough.*

2. What qualities is it important for extreme sportsmen and sportswomen to have?

3. How are extreme sports similar to and dissimilar from other sports?

4. What risks do you think are involved with airborne extreme sports? Use your own ideas as well as the information in the extract.

5. Why do you think someone might want to do a skydive?

## Now try these

1. In your own words, write three different facts about extreme sports. If you can, discover interesting new facts by doing some research.

2. Do extreme sports appeal to you? Write a paragraph to explain why you feel you would or would not be well suited to doing extreme sports, and which sport (if any) you would like to try.

3. Draw a picture of someone taking part in an extreme sport. Label it with information boxes, using details given in the text or from your own research. Use the diagram in the extract as a model.

# Non-fiction (information text): 'What is the Sun?' and Poetry: 'What is the Sun?'

In this unit we explore two different ways of describing the sun – in a non-fiction text and in a poem.

**What is the Sun?**

The sun is a star. It is the nearest star to the earth, which is why it seems much bigger than any other star, but really the sun is quite a small star. Some stars that are much further away are thousands of times bigger than the sun.

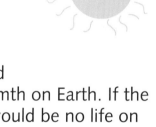

The sun is a huge ball of fiery gas. It is 150 million kilometres from the earth, and without it there would be no light or warmth on Earth. If the sun did not give us light and heat there would be no life on earth, so the sun is very important to us. We are not its only planet, though; it has seven others.

The earth takes about 365 days, or one year, to travel once around the sun.

### 'What is the Sun?'

The Sun is an orange dinghy
sailing across a calm sea.

It is a gold coin
dropped down a drain in heaven.

It is a yellow beach ball
kicked high into the summer sky.

It is a red thumb-print
on a sheet of pale blue paper.

It is the gold top from a milk bottle
floating on a puddle.

**Wes Magee**

## Get started

Copy these sentences carefully and complete them by filling in the gaps. Use the facts and the poem to find the answers.

1. The sun is the nearest star to the_____.

2. The sun is quite a _____ star.

3. Without the sun we would have no
   _____ or _____.

4. According to the poem, the Sun is a yellow
   _____ _____.

5. According to the poem, the sky is like a
   sheet of _____ _____ _____.

## Try these

Write a sentence to answer each question. One has been done for you.

**1.** Why is the sun important to us?

Answer: *The sun is important to us because there would be no light, warmth or life on earth without it.*

**2.** How many metaphors are there in the poem? How many metaphors are there in the non-fiction text?

**3.** The non-fiction text says the sun is made of gas, but the poem suggests the sun is made of gold. Is the sun made of gas or gold? Why do you think this?

**4.** How does the poem describe the sun differently from the non-fiction text?

**5.** Do either of the texts tell you exactly how hot the sun is? Which one do you think would be most likely to tell you? Why do you think this?

## Now try these

**1.** Why does the poem describe the sun differently from the non-fiction text? Write notes about what each writer was trying to do.

**2.** Explain which description of the sun you prefer and why. Which way would you choose to describe the sun to someone who didn't know what it was? Why would you choose this?

**3.** Draw two pictures of the sun. Include the earth in one, and use the details from the non-fiction text to add information boxes. Use ideas from the poem to draw the second picture.

# Poetry: 'Whale Alert'

Teacher said, "Research an animal, in the sea, the air, the ground,"

I chose to find out about the whale and this is what I found.

The whale is peaceful, the whale is smart,
The whale's got a song that could melt your heart.

Whales can't taste, and whales can't smell,
But whales can hear extremely well.

A whale that's singing – folk who know whales say –
Can be heard by others a hundred miles away.

A whale talks with a whistle, a squeak or a click,
Though he's big as a mountain, a whale's very quick.

They have no teeth, so they cannot chew,
And live on fishy things smaller'n me and you.

They never hurt people, so I'm sad to know
That people could treat the poor whale so.

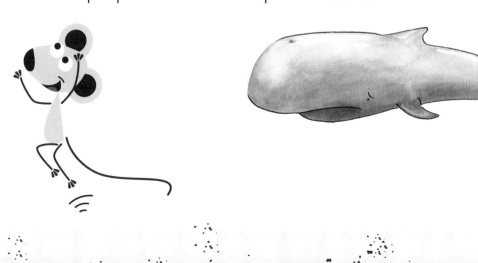

They hunt him for his meat, for his oil and bone,
They will not leave the whale alone.

In just 50 years, two million have died,
Each with a harpoon growing from
its side.

One day, there may be no more whales,
Except those living in fairy tales.

Fairy tales are good places for fairy folk to be,
But whales would be happier living in the sea.

**Valerie Bloom**

## Get started

Copy these lines carefully and complete them by filling in the gaps.
Use the poem to find the answers.

1. Teacher said, "_____ an animal, in the sea, the air, the ground."

2. The whale's got a song that could _____
_____ _____.

3. Whales live on _____ _____ smaller'n me and you.

4. In just _____ _____ , two million whales have died.

5. But whales would be _____ living in the sea.

## Try these

Write a sentence to answer each question. One has been done for you.

1. What task did the teacher set?

   Answer: *The teacher asked the speaker to research an animal.*

2. According to the poem, what can whales do extremely well?

3. According to the poem, why are whales hunted?

4. How do you think the poet feels about whales? Why do you think this?

5. What important message do you think the poem gives the reader?

## Now try these

1. Imagine a whale could put thoughts into words, and write three sentences as though you are a whale. You could consider how it might feel to live in the ocean, to communicate the way a whale does, or to be hunted.

2. Find the eleven pairs of rhyming words. Look at how the rhymes are arranged. Then write four new lines about whales, using the same arrangement of rhymes.

3. Design a poster to raise awareness of the danger faced by whales. Use the poem to help you to add details to your poster.

# Fiction (modern): 'Cave Wars'

**From 'Cave Wars' by Gillian Cross**

Tom and Ruby lived at the seaside, in a house near the beach. In summer, the beach was full of people on holiday, but in winter they all went home. That was when Tom and Ruby played in their secret caves.

There were two caves. The little cave was low down in the cliff, hidden behind thick bushes. The big one was higher up, behind a heap of rocks. No one except Tom and Ruby knew about the caves – until the Gang moved in.

One wet winter afternoon, Tom and Ruby decided to make a camp in the big cave. They set off up the path, with a rug and some sausages, but when they reached the big pile of rocks, they heard voices.

There in the cave were two of the roughest, toughest boys they'd ever seen – and a girl who looked even tougher.

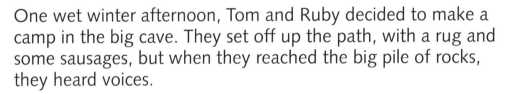

"Hey," shouted Tom, "that's our cave!"

"Not any more!" said the girl.

The boys nodded and pulled horrible faces. "We got here first!" one of them shouted.

Ruby wanted to fight them, but Tom pulled her away. "Don't be silly," he whispered. "They're HUGE!"

He dragged her back down the path to the little cave. She was very, very angry.

"They've stolen our cave," she said. "We've got to *do* something."

There was a piece of old board lying on the beach. Tom stared at it. "I've had an idea," he said.

## Get started

Copy these sentences carefully and complete them by filling in the gaps. Use the story to find the answers.

1. Tom and Ruby lived at the _____, in a house near the beach.

2. The big one was higher up, behind a _____ _____ _____.

3. One wet winter afternoon, Tom and Ruby _____ to make a camp in the big cave.

4. The boys nodded and pulled _____ _____.

5. There was a piece of old _____ lying on the beach.

## Try these

Write a sentence to answer each question. One has been done for you.

1. What did Tom and Ruby take with them to the beach?

    Answer: *Tom and Ruby took a rug and some sausages to the beach.*

2. Where are the two caves described in the story?

3. When did Tom and Ruby play in the secret caves? Why do you think they didn't play in them all year round?

4. How did Ruby feel about the other children in the cave? How do you know?

5. Do you think it is fair for Ruby to call the bigger cave 'our cave'? Why or why not?

## Now try these

1. The extract describes Ruby as being very, very angry, but it does not describe Tom's feelings. Write three sentences as though Tom is thinking them, to describe how he feels.

2. What do you think Tom's idea could be? Write the next paragraph in the story, using your ideas.

3. Draw a detailed picture of Tom and Ruby discovering the other children in the cave.

# Playscript: 'Sophie's Rules'

**From 'Sophie's Rules' by Keith West**

### SCENE 1

(Dana's new to Deepvale School. She notices Sophie, Anna and Jade. They're sitting in the classroom, having arrived early. She walks nervously up to them.)

**DANA:** (shyly)
  Hi.

**SOPHIE:** (turning round to look at Dana)
  Hi. What are you doing in our classroom? You new here?

**DANA:** Yes, I'm Dana. I've just arrived here – we've just moved in. What's your name?

**SOPHIE:** My name's Sophie and my mates are Anna (pointing to the other girl) and Jade.

**ANNA:** You can sit with us if you like.

(Sophie scowls.)

**DANA:** (enthusiastically) Thanks!

**SOPHIE:** I can tell you're not from round here. You're different.

**DANA:** Mum and I have just moved into Wordsworth Crescent.

**SOPHIE:** (smirking)
  Wordsworth Crescent?

**JADE:** Isn't that where Natalie Shanks lives?

**SOPHIE:** *(nastily)*
Longshanks, sheepshanks.
*(to Dana)*
She's weird. We don't like people from Wordsworth Crescent, *(to Jade and Anna)* do we?

*(Dana looks nervous and swallows hard.)*

**JADE:** No.

**ANNA:** We don't.

**SOPHIE:** *(pointing at Dana's clothes)*
Why aren't you in school uniform, like us? I wouldn't be seen dead in what you're wearing.

*(Dana looks down at her clothes.)*

**JADE:** *(nastily)*
Yeah, what's so special about you? Why do you have to be different?

**DANA:** Because –

**JADE:** Because you're from Wordsworth Crescent, that's why. They're all nerds down that part of town.

## Get started

Copy these sentences carefully and complete them by filling in the gaps. Use the playscript to find the answers.

1. Dana's new to _____ School.

2. She notices Sophie, Anna and _____.

3. I can tell you're not from _____ _____.

**4.** We don't like people from _____ Crescent.

**5.** Why aren't you in _____ _____, like us?

## Try these

Write a sentence to answer each question. One has been done for you.

**1.** Who invites Dana to sit down with the girls?

Answer: *Anna says that Dana can sit with them if she likes.*

**2.** How does Sophie say she can tell Dana isn't from 'round here'?

**3.** How does Sophie feel when Anna invites Dana to sit down? How do you know?

**4.** Do you think Sophie, Anna and Jade all feel the same way about Dana? What makes you think that?

**5.** Look at the layout of the playscript. What features does it have that tell you it is a playscript rather than a story?

## Now try these

**1.** How might Dana have felt during the conversation? Write a short diary entry as Dana, describing the events in the extract. Try to imagine how her feelings may have changed by the time she writes the diary entry, too.

**2.** What do you think happens next in the playscript? What do you think Dana says or does? What would you do? Write a paragraph to explain your ideas.

**3.** Draw a picture of the scene. Try to show the characters' feelings through their positions, body language and facial expressions.

# Non-fiction (information text): 'Black Holes'

**From 'Black Holes' by Anna Claybourne**

**Dark stars**

When telescopes were invented in 1609, scientists pointed them at the sky and began to find out much more about space. Italian scientist Galileo used an early telescope to see Saturn's rings and Jupiter's moons, and he discovered that the Milky Way was made of billions of stars.

In 1784, a scientist called John Michell wrote about strange objects in space that swallowed light. He said that you could not see these objects, but he knew that they could make other stars move in a strange way. He called these objects "dark stars", but it was not until the 20th century that scientists found signs that dark stars really do exist. Today, we call them black holes.

**What are black holes?**

Black holes aren't actually holes. They don't lead anywhere – you can't go through a black hole and end up somewhere else.

A black hole is more like a tiny, invisible point in space, which works like a powerful plughole. Objects that come close to a black hole get pulled towards it, then disappear into it – whether they're very small, like dust, or large, like rocks. Black holes can even swallow whole moons, planets and stars. If a spaceship flew too close to a black hole, it would get pulled in too. So would you, if you were floating past in a spacesuit.

## Get started

Copy these sentences carefully and complete them by filling in the gaps. Use the facts to find the answers.

1. Telescopes were _____ in 1609.

2. Galileo discovered that the _____ _____ was made of billions of stars.

3. John Michell wrote about strange objects that _____ light.

4. Black holes aren't _____ holes.

5. A black hole is like a tiny, invisible _____ in _____.

## Try these

Write a sentence to answer each question. One has been done for you.

1. What did Galileo look at through his telescope?

   Answer: *Galileo used his telescope to look at Saturn's rings and Jupiter's moons.*

2. What did scientists discover in the 20th century?

3. How did John Michell describe the way 'dark stars' look?

4. Do you think that comparing a black hole to a powerful plughole helps the reader to understand what a black hole is like? Why or why not?

5. Why do you think it might be difficult to find out more about black holes?

## Now try these

1. How do you think Galileo might have felt when he made his discoveries? Write three sentences as though you are Galileo, to share your thoughts.

2. In your own words, write three different facts about black holes. If you can, discover interesting new facts by doing some research.

3. Draw a timeline to show the development from the invention of telescopes to the discovery of black holes, including the dates you are given in the extract. If you can, research other astronomical events to add to your timeline.

# Fiction (modern): 'Tiger Dead! Tiger Dead!'

**From 'Tiger Dead! Tiger Dead!' by Grace Nichols**

**Chapter 1**

One day Tiger was strolling through the forest and stopping every few moments to admire his stripy face in a stream. Times were hard and suddenly an idea came to Tiger's head that it would be nice to have the forest all to himself. To himself and his family of course.

The more Tiger thought about it, the more he fell in love with the idea, until he began to speak his feelings aloud: "Imagine me roving freely. Me and my family will have all this to ourselves. No Monkey, Snake, Turtle and the rest to pester me. I must think of a plan to get rid of them, especially that troublesome spider-person who calls himself Anansi. I will play dead to catch the living."

Tiger was so taken up with himself that he didn't see Anansi himself sitting on top of a palm tree. Anansi, that tricky little spider-man, was the last person Tiger would have wanted to overhear him.

And guess what? Anansi had listened to every single word.

Well, as soon as Tiger got home he told his wife about the plan he had to become king of the jungle.

The plan was simple. He, Tiger, would pretend to be dead and all the animals would be invited to his home. His wife would allow them, one by one, to go into a back room and see the body. As each animal passed by, he, Tiger, would rise up and hit each one down with a big stick.

## Get started

Copy these sentences carefully and complete them by filling in the gaps. Use the story to find the answers.

1. One day Tiger was _____ through the forest.

2. Times were _____ and suddenly an idea came to Tiger's head.

3. Tiger didn't see _____ _____ sitting on top of a palm trcc.

4. Anansi had _____ to every single word.

5. Well, as soon as Tiger got home he told his _____ about the _____ he had to become king of the jungle.

## Try these

Write a sentence to answer each question. One has been done for you.

1. Why did Tiger keep stopping every few moments?

   Answers: *Tiger kept stopping every few moments to admire his stripy face in a stream.*

2. What was the idea that came to Tiger's head?

3. How did Tiger feel about his idea?

4. What is Anansi like? How do you think he is likely to act? Why do you think this?

5. How would you describe Tiger's personality?

## Now try these

1. How do you think Tiger's wife felt, hearing Tiger's idea and plan? Write three sentences as though Tiger's wife is thinking them.

2. Rewrite the extract from Anansi's point of view.

3. Draw a detailed picture of Tiger strolling through the forest. Use the extract to help you. Use speech bubbles to show what he is saying.

# Poetry: 'Feeding the Ducks'

**Feeding the Ducks**

We're off to feed the ducks,

The ducks, the ducks.

We're off to feed the ducks,

Hear them quacking in the rain.

What shall we feed the ducks?

The ducks, the ducks?

What shall we feed the ducks?

Soggy bread means tummy pain.

Snails and slugs and insects,

Worms and hard-boiled eggs,

Turnip-tops and lettuce,

Acorns, seed and grain.

We've been to feed the ducks,

The ducks, the ducks.

We've been to feed the ducks,

And they quacked "Please come again."

**Roger McGough**

## Get started

Copy these sentences carefully and complete them by filling in the gaps. Use the poem to find the answers.

1. We're off to _____ the _____.
2. Hear them _____ in the _____.
3. What _____ we feed the _____?
4. Soggy _____ means _____ pain.
5. Snails and slugs and _____,
   Worms and _____ - _____ _____.

## Try these

Write a sentence to answer each question. One has been done for you.

1. What is the speaker going to do?
   Answer: *The speaker is going to feed ducks.*
2. What does the poem suggest that ducks should eat?
3. Why shouldn't ducks eat soggy bread?
4. Who exactly do you think is going to feed the ducks in the poem?
5. Which parts of the poem are repeated? What effect do you think this has on the reader?

## Now try these

1. How do you think the poet feels about the ducks? How do you know? Write three sentences as though you are the poet, to explain how you feel.
2. Find the rhyming words in the poem. Look at how the rhymes are arranged. Then write two new verses about the ducks, using the same arrangement of rhymes.
3. Draw a picture of the ducks being fed. Use the poem to make your drawing detailed.